SEEING *Christ* IN *Christmas*

DIETER F. UCHTDORF

DESERET
BOOK

SALT LAKE CITY, UTAH

ISBN 978-1-62972-467-6

Printed in the United States of America
Sun Print Solutions, Salt Lake City, UT

10 9 8 7 6 5 4 3 2

After the end of World War II, my family lived for a time in Zwickau, East Germany—that is where we found and joined The Church of Jesus Christ of Latter-day Saints. Our congregation met in a small villa that had been converted into a meetinghouse, and there we joined with other members of the Church in worshipping the Savior and renewing our baptismal covenants.

One of the most striking things about our chapel was its beautiful stained-glass window depicting the Savior and the visit of our Heavenly Father and His Son to the Prophet Joseph Smith. As a young boy, I often looked up at this window and felt a special spirit. How I loved our quaint meetinghouse!

The special feeling in this building seemed to be enhanced during Christmastime. Somehow the smells were sweeter, the sounds were softer, the lights were more enchanting as they reflected off the stained-glass windows during those dark winter evenings. I will never forget this little villa because of the spirit I felt within its walls.

Years later, I grieved when I learned that this much-loved chapel—the place that had cradled us in its arms during the first years of our Church membership—had been demolished to make room for a high-rise apartment building.

I would think that those who made the decision to take down the building had good intentions and did not know what this villa meant to our small flock. To them it probably looked like just another building. Had they been able to see it as a house of worship, a place of rejoicing and friendship, a sacred chapel—had they only seen the place the way I did as a young child, they might have made a different decision.

I like the novel *Le petit prince* by Antoine de Saint-Exupéry. It contains this keen observation: "Grown-ups never understand anything by themselves, and it is exhausting for children to have to provide explanations over and over again."[1] Later in the story a wise fox explains another important truth to the little prince: "Here is my secret. It's quite simple: One sees clearly only with the heart. Anything essential is invisible to the eyes."[2]

Not being able to see the sacred either with the eyes or with the heart has been a fault of the human condition since the beginning. In the scriptures we read, "For the things which some men esteem to be of great worth, . . . others set at naught and trample under their feet."[3] Sometimes the most precious and sacred things are right in front of us—in plain sight, so to speak—but we cannot or will not see them.

This may be especially true during the blessed and precious season of Christmas. This is a beautiful time of the year. Trees are draped with lovely sparkling lights, the stores glitter with dazzling decorations, and the streets bustle with crowds of shoppers seeking gifts for those they love.

All of these spectacular displays and decorations that compete for our attention can be beautiful and uplifting, but if that's all we see, then we're missing something that's in plain sight. Sometimes, despite our best intentions, we become so preoccupied with responsibilities, commitments, and the stress of our many tasks that we fail to see with our hearts that which is essential and most sacred.

Even many who lived during the time of the Savior's

mortal ministry could not see Him, though He walked among them in plain sight.

WHY COULDN'T THEY SEE HIM?

Jesus Christ was born in a stable surrounded by lowly animals. He was raised in a disparaged town on the fringes of civilization. He did not go through the pattern of worldly education. He was not trained in worldly schools of philosophy, art, or literature. Some who heard His teachings questioned the origins of His education, saying, "How knoweth this man letters, having never learned?"[4] and they said also, "Whence hath this man [his] wisdom? . . . Is not this the carpenter's son? is not his mother called Mary? and his brethren . . . and his sisters, are they not all with us? Whence then hath this man all these things?"[5]

The sophisticated and the proud, those who placed their trust in worldly learning, could not see Him.

Jesus the Christ was not wealthy, nor did He hold a political office. He lived and taught among humble people in a nation that was in bondage to the Romans. Therefore He did not seem worthy of notice by the political leaders of the day. They were, after all, preoccupied with running the world. They were far too busy to pay attention to a humble preacher of righteousness.

When Jesus stood before Pilate, the powerful Roman governor could see only a teacher who was the cause of a disturbance in his political jurisdiction.

The wealthy and the influential, those who were caught up in their busy affairs of commerce and government, could not see Him.

The scribes and Pharisees and other religious leaders of the day were looking for the Messiah. They had studied the scriptures and longed for the time of the coming of the One who would deliver Israel. They yearned to see His day. They prayed for His arrival.

But they were so steeped in their own traditions and so blinded by their own narrow interpretation of scripture that they could not see the humble man who walked among them.

Jesus did not come in the way they expected. He had not attended their religious schools. Worse, He did not agree with all of their teachings and, therefore, He could not be the One.

The self-righteous and unteachable, those whose hearts were closed to the Spirit, could not see Him.

But Who Saw Him?

Simeon, an elderly, devout, and just man, saw the Christ. When Mary and Joseph brought the baby Jesus to the temple, Simeon knew through the power of the Holy Ghost that this was indeed the Christ, the Son of the Most High. And he took the baby in his arms and blessed Him.[6]

Humble fishermen and laborers saw Him. The ailing, the humble, and the distraught saw Him and recognized Him as the Salvation of Israel. But there were those among the rich and powerful who were teachable and therefore could see the Christ. Nicodemus, a ruler of the Jews, saw Him,[7] as did the wealthy Joseph of Arimathea[8] and Zacchaeus the publican.[9]

Now, Can We See the Christ?

Sometimes when we read about people who could not see the Savior for who He was, we marvel at their blindness. But do *we* also let distractions obstruct our view of the Savior—during this Christmas season and throughout the year? Some are external distractions—the gifts we worry about, the decorations, or the clamorous advertising—but often it is what is inside us that blinds us from seeing the Christ.

Some may feel a certain level of intellectual aloofness that distances them from Christ. In an age when vast amounts of knowledge are at our fingertips, the familiar story of Jesus the Christ can get lost amid the flood of scientific advances, pressing news, or the latest popular movies or books.

Some are so caught up in the details of running their lives that they don't make time for much else. They might pay lip service to the things of the Spirit, but their hearts are so focused on the world that they cannot see the Christ.

Some, like the Pharisees, seek for the Christ, but their hearts are so set upon their own theories, spiritual hobbies, and opinions that they fail to recognize Him. In spite of their good intentions, they miss the transforming revelations of the Holy Spirit and thereby miss the only way to receive a certain testimony of Jesus Christ.

LET US SEE THE CHRIST IN CHRISTMAS

This is a season of rejoicing! A season of celebration! A wonderful time when we acknowledge that our Almighty God sent His Only Begotten Son, Jesus Christ, to redeem the world! To redeem us!

It is a season of charitable acts of kindness and brotherly love. It is a season of being more reflective about our own lives and about the many blessings that are ours. It is a season of forgiving and being forgiven.

But perhaps most of all, let it be a season of seeking

the Lamb of God, the King of Glory, the Everlasting Light of the World, the Great Hope of Mankind, the Savior and Redeemer of our souls.

I promise that if we unclutter our lives a little bit and in sincerity and humility seek the pure and gentle Christ with our hearts, we will see Him, we will find Him—on Christmas and throughout the year.

Notes

1. Antoine de Saint-Exupéry, *The Little Prince,* trans. by Richard Howard (New York: Mariner Books, 2000), 2.
2. Antoine de Saint-Exupéry, *The Little Prince,* 63.
3. 1 Nephi 19:7.
4. John 7:15.
5. Matthew 13:54–56.
6. See Luke 2:25–35.
7. See John 3:1–21.
8. See Matthew 27:57–58.
9. See Luke 19:2–10.

About the Author

Elder Dieter F. Uchtdorf was sustained as a member of the Quorum of the Twelve Apostles of the Church in 2004. He was called as second counselor in the First Presidency of The Church of Jesus Christ of Latter-day Saints in 2008 and served in that position until 2018. He has served as a General Authority since 1994.

Elder Uchtdorf was born on November 6, 1940, in Ostrava, Czechoslovakia, to Karl Albert and Hildegard Opelt Uchtdorf. In 1947 his family became members of the Church in Zwickau, Germany. They fled to Frankfurt/Main in 1952, where he received an education in engineering. In 1959 he joined the German Air Force and served for six years as a fighter pilot.

In 1965 Elder Uchtdorf began working for Lufthansa German Airlines as a pilot. From 1970 until 1996 he flew as captain of several aircraft, including the Boeing 747. While also working as training and check captain, he received several management responsibilities, culminating in being named

Senior Vice President Flight Operations and Lufthansa Chief Pilot.

He married Harriet Reich in 1962. They have two children, six grandchildren, and one great-grandchild. With his call as an Apostle, Elder Uchtdorf and his family left their homeland and now live permanently in the United States.

Dieter and Harriet Uchtdorf enjoy outdoor activities, cherish the arts, and are happiest when spending time with their family.